Welcome To

THE COMPLETE GUIDE TO CHOOSING THE BEST BABY NAME FOR 2023

BY MAYA EVELYN M.E

WITHOUT A DOUBT, CHOOSING A BABY NAME IS ONE OF THE BIGGEST DECISIONS THAT NEW PARENTS WILL MAKE. AND RIGHTFULLY SO! YOUR BABY IS GOING TO CARRY THE NAME YOU CHOOSE FOR THEM THROUGHOUT THEIR ENTIRE LIFE. SO, IT ISN'T REALLY SOMETHING THAT YOU WANT TO TAKE LIGHTLY. NO PARENT WANTS TO END UP WITH BABY NAME REMORSE! THE GOOD NEWS IS, WE CAN HELP! WE ARE GOING TO WALK YOU THROUGH 5 SIMPLE STEPS TO CHOOSING A BABY NAME THAT YOU'LL LOVE!

This book contains :

- Simple Steps to Choosing a Baby Name
- Websites and tools to help you
- Top 200 Baby Names
- +2000 Baby Names
- Work Pages

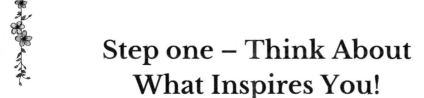

Step one – Think About What Inspires You!

THE BEST FIRST STEP IS TO START BY THINKING ABOUT THE BABY NAMES THAT INSPIRE YOU AND YOUR FAMILY. YOU CAN START BY LOOKING AT YOUR FAMILY CULTURE, PERHAPS THE REAL BABY NAMES OF GRANDPARENTS OR GREAT-GRANDPARENTS, THINGS THAT MAKE YOU FEEL GOOD ABOUT YOURSELF AND THE PEOPLE WHO INSPIRE YOU, OR EVEN YOUR FAVORITE CHARACTERS FROM BOOKS OR MOVIES!

HERE ARE A FEW QUESTIONS YOU CAN ASK YOURSELF TO DETERMINE WHAT IS AN IMPORTANT INFLUENCE IN YOUR BABY'S NAME DECISION:

- IS FAMILY CULTURE OF IMPORTANCE TO YOU?
- DO YOU WANT TO HONOR A LOVED ONE OR PERSON OF INFLUENCE? AND IF YES, WHAT ARE THE WAYS YOU CAN HONOR THEM I.E. THEIR NAME, SOMETHING THAT REMINDS YOU OF THEM
- DO YOU WANT TO THEME YOUR BABY NAME?
- DO YOU WANT TO THEME CURRENT OR FUTURE SIBLING NAMES?
- IS THE NAME'S MEANING IMPORTANT TO YOU?
- WHAT ARE THE THINGS THAT YOU AND/OR YOUR FAMILY ARE DRAWN TO?
- DO YOU WANT A NAME THAT IS TIMELESS OR TRENDY?
- DO YOU WANT THE NAME TO IMPLY A CERTAIN FEELING OR REACTION I.E. CUTE, STRONG, BEAUTIFUL, PREPPY
- WHAT DO YOU WANT YOUR BABY'S NAME TO SAY ABOUT THEM?

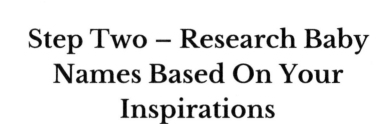

Step Two – Research Baby Names Based On Your Inspirations

ONCE YOU HAVE IDENTIFIED THE THINGS THAT INSPIRE YOU, IT'S TIME TO BEGIN RESEARCHING. SPECIFICALLY, YOU WANT TO SEARCH FOR YOUR TOPICS ON GOOGLE. FIRST, BE VERY SPECIFIC ABOUT WHAT YOU WANT AND SEARCH FOR 'GIRL NAMES THAT MEAN ROYAL' OR 'ROYAL GIRL NAMES'. THEN, WHILE YOU ARE BROWSING THROUGH THE VARIOUS NAMES MAKE SURE TO JOT DOWN THOSE YOU LIKE OR STAND OUT TO YOU.

THERE IS NOTHING WORSE THAN SEEING A NAME YOU LIKE, ONLY TO FORGET IT A FEW MINUTES LATER AND NOT BEING ABLE TO FIND IT AGAIN!

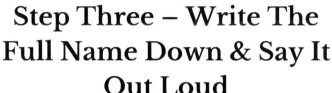

Step Three – Write The Full Name Down & Say It Out Loud

NOW YOU HAVE A FEW NAMES ON YOUR LIST, THE NEXT STEP IS TO START PUTTING THE FULL NAME TOGETHER WITH ANY POTENTIAL MIDDLE NAMES AND LAST NAMES.

YOU'RE GOING TO WANT TO SEE IF YOU LIKE THE WAY IT LOOKS WHEN IT IS WRITTEN.

ASK YOURSELF:

1 DO YOU LIKE THE WAY IT LOOKS TOGETHER?
2 IS IT TOO SHORT?
3 IS IT TOO LONG?
4 DO THE INITIALS OR MONOGRAMS SPELL SOMETHING UNTOWARD? YOU PROBABLY DON'T WANT THE INITIALS TO SPELL OUT B.U.M., A.S.S., F.M.L, W.T.F, OR SIMILAR. AND IF YOU'RE NOT SURE WE RECOMMEND DOING A QUICK GOOGLE SEARCH.
5 WHAT CAN THE NAME BE SHORTENED TO? PEOPLE LOVE TO SHORTEN NAMES, SO MAKE SURE YOU ALSO LIKE THE POTENTIALLY SHORTEN VERSION. OR AT LEAST BE AWARE THAT YOU MAY NEED TO SET BOUNDARIES FROM THE GET-GO.
6 DOES THE NAME OR SHORTENED VERSION OF THE NAME RHYME WITH ANYTHING OR CAN BE USED IN A WAY THAT YOUR CHILD MAY BE TEASED? FOR EXAMPLE, 'FATTIE PATTIE'.

Step four – Research The Full Name

HOPEFULLY, BY NOW YOU HAVE STARTED TO NARROW DOWN YOUR NAME CHOICES AND MIGHT HAVE EVEN PICKED YOUR TOP 2 OR 3 CHOICES. SO, IT'S TIME TO DO A LITTLE MORE RESEARCH! FIRST, YOU WANT TO FIND OUT WHAT THE BABY NAME MEANS. YOU CAN DO THIS BY TYPING THE NAME   MEANING INTO A GOOGLE SEARCH.

THE NEXT THING YOU NEED TO DO IS SEARCH THE FULL NAME ON GOOGLE. THIS WILL HELP YOU SEE IF THERE ARE ANY NEGATIVE CONNOTATIONS THAT MAY DETER YOU FROM LOVING THE NAME. YOU WANT TO SEE IF IT'S THE NAME OF A FAMOUS CELEBRITY OR EVEN A SERIAL KILLER? IS IT A WELL KNOWN SONG?

Step five – Let The Name Sit With You

CONGRATULATIONS! IF YOU'VE MADE IT TO THIS STEP, NO DOUBT YOU HAVE NARROWED DOWN YOUR BABY NAME CHOICES TO JUST A FEW. YOU MAY HAVE EVEN CHOSEN YOUR PERFECT BABY NAME! BUT DON'T STRESS IF YOU ARE STILL UNDECIDED. SOMETIMES IT JUST TAKES TIME TO LET THEM SIT WITH YOU FOR A LITTLE WHILE BEFORE MAKING YOUR FINAL DECISION.

Use a Baby Name Website to Help Your Search

USE A BABY NAME WEBSITE TO HELP YOU FIND THE PERFECT NAME FOR YOUR NEW BUNDLE OF JOY.

THIS IS A USER FRIENDLY SEARCH ENGINE WHERE YOU CAN EASILY FIND SOME GORGEOUS BABY NAMES FOR BOTH GIRLS AND BOYS. MAKE YOUR OWN ACCOUNT AND YOU CAN BUILD YOUR OWN SHORT LIST RIGHT THERE ON THE WEBSITE.

GREAT SITE, I RECOMMEND IT

JUST SCAN QR

SITE 1

SITE 2

ALL WE CARE ABOUT IS GUIDING YOU AND HELPING YOU
CHOOSE YOUR CHILD'S NAME, AND WE WILL BE VERY
HAPPY WITH THAT. THEREFORE, IF YOU DO NOT FIND WHAT
YOU WANT IN THIS BOOK, WE STILL HELP DIRECT YOU TO
SOURCES THAT WE HOPE WILL HELP YOU.

TOP BABY GIRLS
NAMES OF 2023

1 OLIVIA ⬭

2 EMMA ⬭

3 AMELIA ⬭

4 AVA ⬭

5 SOPHIA ⬭

6 ISABELLA ⬭

7 LUNA ⬭

8 MIA ⬭

9 CHARLOTTE ⬭

10 EVELYN ⬭

11 HARPER ⬭

12 SCARLETT ⬭

13 NOVA ⬭

14 AURORA ⬭

15 ELLA ⬭

16 MILA ⬭

17 ARIA ⬭

18 ELLIE ⬭

19 GIANNA ⬭

20 SOFIA ⬭

21 VIOLET ⬭
22 LAYLA ⬭
23 WILLOW ⬭
24 LILY ⬭
25 HAZEL ⬭
26 CAMILA ⬭
27 AVERY ⬭
28 CHLOE ⬭
29 ELENA ⬭
30 PAISLEY ⬭
31 ELIANA ⬭
32 PENELOPE ⬭
33 ELEANOR ⬭
34 IVY ⬭
35 ELIZABETH ⬭
36 RILEY ⬭
37 ISLA ⬭
38 ABIGAIL ⬭
39 NORA ⬭
40 STELLA ⬭

41 GRACE ⬭
42 ZOEY ⬭
43 EMILY ⬭
44 EMILIA ⬭
45 LEILANI ⬭
46 EVERLY ⬭
47 KINSLEY ⬭
48 ATHENA ⬭
49 DELILAH ⬭
50 NAOMI ⬭
51 MAYA ⬭
52 MADISON ⬭
53 LUCY ⬭
54 ADDISON ⬭
55 ZOE ⬭
56 BELLA ⬭
57 VICTORIA ⬭
58 ALICE ⬭
59 SOPHIE ⬭
60 EVERLEIGH ⬭

61 HANNAH ⬭
62 AALIYAH ⬭
63 NATALIE ⬭
64 ARYA ⬭
65 AYLA ⬭
66 IRIS ⬭
67 AUTUMN ⬭
68 RAELYNN ⬭
69 VALENTINA ⬭
70 SERENITY ⬭
71 SKYLAR ⬭
72 RYLEE ⬭
73 NEVAEH ⬭
74 LILLIAN ⬭
75 AUDREY ⬭
76 EVA ⬭
77 MADELYN ⬭
78 LEAH ⬭
79 KENNEDY ⬭
80 BROOKLYN ⬭

81 SADIE ⬭

82 HAILEY ⬭

83 CLAIRE ⬭

84 SAVANNAH ⬭

85 RUBY ⬭

86 EMERY ⬭

87 AUBREY ⬭

88 GABRIELLA ⬭

89 MELODY ⬭

90 MARIA ⬭

91 BRIELLE ⬭

92 AMARA ⬭

93 FREYA ⬭

94 ARIANA ⬭

95 LYLA ⬭

96 ANNA ⬭

97 PIPER ⬭

98 SARAH ⬭

99 JADE ⬭

100 ADELINE ⬭

TOP BABY BOYS
NAMES OF 2023

1 LIAM ⬭
2 NOAH ⬭
3 OLIVER ⬭
4 ELIJAH ⬭
5 MATEO ⬭
6 LUCAS ⬭
7 LEVI ⬭
8 ASHER ⬭
9 JAMES ⬭
10 LEO ⬭
11 GRAYSON ⬭
12 EZRA ⬭
13 LUCA ⬭
14 ETHAN ⬭
15 AIDEN ⬭
16 WYATT ⬭
17 SEBASTIAN ⬭
18 BENJAMIN ⬭
19 MASON ⬭
20 HENRY ⬭

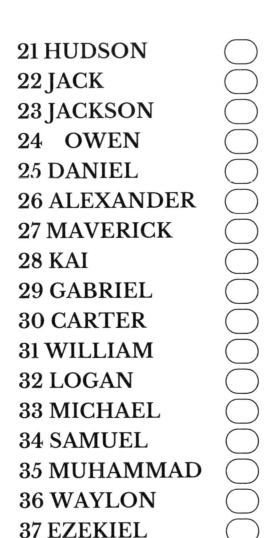

21 HUDSON ◯
22 JACK ◯
23 JACKSON ◯
24 OWEN ◯
25 DANIEL ◯
26 ALEXANDER ◯
27 MAVERICK ◯
28 KAI ◯
29 GABRIEL ◯
30 CARTER ◯
31 WILLIAM ◯
32 LOGAN ◯
33 MICHAEL ◯
34 SAMUEL ◯
35 MUHAMMAD ◯
36 WAYLON ◯
37 EZEKIEL ◯
38 JAYDEN ◯
39 LUKE ◯
40 LINCOLN ◯

61 GREYSON	⬭
62 JOSEPH	⬭
63 KAYDEN	⬭
64 SANTIAGO	⬭
65 JAMESON	⬭
66 ADRIAN	⬭
67 MILES	⬭
68 COLTON	⬭
69 NOLAN	⬭
70 ROMAN	⬭
71 HUNTER	⬭
72 JACE	⬭
73 EASTON	⬭
74 CHRISTOPHER	⬭
75 MYLES	⬭
76 LANDON	⬭
77 MICAH	⬭
78 JEREMIAH	⬭
79 XAVIER	⬭
80 RIVER	⬭

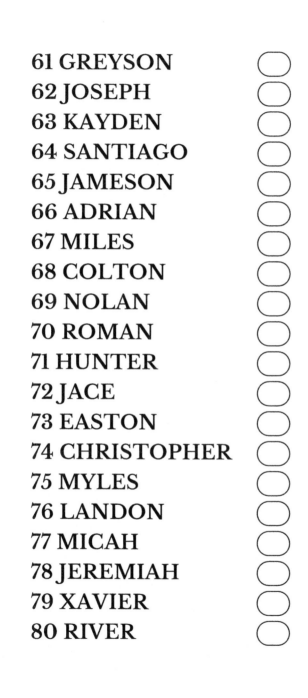

81 SILAS ◯
82 CHRISTIAN ◯
83 JOSHUA ◯
84 WESTON ◯
85 JORDAN ◯
86 LEGEND ◯
87 JAXSON ◯
88 PARKER ◯
89 CAMERON ◯
90 DYLAN ◯
91 KINGSTON ◯
92 RYDER ◯
93 CHARLIE ◯
94 EVERETT ◯
95 ANDREW ◯
96 DECLAN ◯
97 LUKA ◯
98 ZION ◯
99 WESLEY ◯
100 ATLAS ◯

+2000
Baby Names List

Baby Girl Names list

• Olivia	◯	• Emily	◯
• Emma	◯	• Aria	◯
• Charlotte	◯	• Penelope	◯
• Amelia	◯	• Chloe	◯
• Ava	◯	• Layla	◯
• Sophia	◯	• Mila	◯
• Isabella	◯	• Nora	◯
• Mia	◯	• Hazel	◯
• Evelyn	◯	• Madison	◯
• Harper	◯	• Ellie	◯
• Luna	◯	• Lily	◯
• Camila	◯	• Nova	◯
• Gianna	◯	• Isla	◯
• Elizabeth	◯	• Grace	◯
• Eleanor	◯	• Violet	◯
• Ella	◯	• Aurora	◯
• Abigail	◯	• Riley	◯
• Sofia	◯	• Zoey	◯
• Avery	◯	• Willow	◯
• Scarlett	◯	• Emilia	◯

- Stella ◯
- Zoe ◯
- Victoria ◯
- Hannah ◯
- Addison ◯
- Leah ◯
- Lucy ◯
- Eliana ◯
- Ivy ◯
- Everly ◯
- Lillian ◯
- Paisley ◯
- Elena ◯
- Naomi ◯
- Maya ◯
- Natalie ◯
- Kinsley ◯
- Delilah ◯
- Claire ◯
- Audrey ◯

- Aaliyah ◯
- Ruby ◯
- Brooklyn ◯
- Alice ◯
- Aubrey ◯
- Autumn ◯
- Leilani ◯
- Savannah ◯
- Valentina ◯
- Kennedy ◯
- Madelyn ◯
- Josephine ◯
- Bella ◯
- Skylar ◯
- Genesis ◯
- Sophie ◯
- Hailey ◯
- Sadie ◯
- Natalia ◯
- Quinn ◯

- Caroline ◯
- Allison ◯
- Gabriella ◯
- Anna ◯
- Serenity ◯
- Nevaeh ◯
- Cora ◯
- Ariana ◯
- Emery ◯
- Lydia ◯
- Jade ◯
- Sarah ◯
- Eva ◯
- Adeline ◯
- Madeline ◯
- Piper ◯
- Rylee ◯
- Athena ◯
- Peyton ◯
- Everleigh ◯

- Vivian ◯
- Clara ◯
- Raelynn ◯
- Liliana ◯
- Samantha ◯
- Maria ◯
- Iris ◯
- Ayla ◯
- Eloise ◯
- Lyla ◯
- Eliza ◯
- Hadley ◯
- Melody ◯
- Julia ◯
- Parker ◯
- Rose ◯
- Isabelle ◯
- Brielle ◯
- Adalynn ◯
- Arya ◯

- Eden ○
- Remi ○
- Mackenzie ○
- Maeve ○
- Margaret ○
- Reagan ○
- Charlie ○
- Alaia ○
- Melanie ○
- Josie ○
- Elliana ○
- Cecilia ○
- Mary ○
- Daisy ○
- Alina ○
- Lucia ○
- Ximena ○
- Juniper ○
- Kaylee ○
- Magnolia ○

- Summer ○
- Adalyn ○
- Sloane ○
- Amara ○
- Arianna ○
- Isabel ○
- Reese ○
- Emersyn ○
- Sienna ○
- Kehlani ○
- River ○
- Freya ○
- Valerie ○
- Blakely ○
- Genevieve ○
- Esther ○
- Valeria ○
- Katherine ○
- Kylie ○
- Norah ○

• Amaya	○	• Anastasia	○
• Bailey	○	• Olive	○
• Ember	○	• Alani	○
• Ryleigh	○	• Brianna	○
• Georgia	○	• Rosalie	○
• Catalina	○	• Molly	○
• Emerson	○	• Brynlee	○
• Alexandra	○	• Amy	○
• Faith	○	• Ruth	○
• Jasmine	○	• Aubree	○
• Ariella	○	• Gemma	○
• Ashley	○	• Taylor	○
• Andrea	○	• Oakley	○
• Millie	○	• Margot	○
• June	○	• Arabella	○
• Khloe	○	• Sara	○
• Callie	○	• Journee	○
• Juliette	○	• Harmony	○
• Sage	○	• Blake	○
• Ada	○	• Alaina	○

- Aspen ◯
- Noelle ◯
- Selena ◯
- Oaklynn ◯
- Morgan ◯
- Londyn ◯
- Zuri ◯
- Aliyah ◯
- Jordyn ◯
- Juliana ◯
- Finley ◯
- Presley ◯
- Zara ◯
- Leila ◯
- Marley ◯
- Sawyer ◯
- Amira ◯
- Lilly ◯
- London ◯
- Kimberly ◯

- Elsie ◯
- Ariel ◯
- Lila ◯
- Alana ◯
- Diana ◯
- Kamila ◯
- Nyla ◯
- Vera ◯
- Hope ◯
- Annie ◯
- Kaia ◯
- Myla ◯
- Alyssa ◯
- Angela ◯
- Ana ◯
- Lennon ◯
- Evangeline ◯
- Harlow ◯
- Rachel ◯
- Gracie ◯

- Rowan ○
- Laila ○
- Elise ○
- Sutton ○
- Lilah ○
- Adelyn ○
- Phoebe ○
- Octavia ○
- Sydney ○
- Mariana ○
- Wren ○
- Lainey ○
- Vanessa ○
- Teagan ○
- Kayla ○
- Malia ○
- Elaina ○
- Saylor ○
- Brooke ○
- Lola ○

- Miriam ○
- Alayna ○
- Adelaide ○
- Daniela ○
- Jane ○
- Payton ○
- Journey ○
- Lilith ○
- Delaney ○
- Dakota ○
- Mya ○
- Charlee ○
- Alivia ○
- Annabelle ○
- Kailani ○
- Lucille ○
- Trinity ○
- Gia ○
- Tatum ○
- Raegan ○

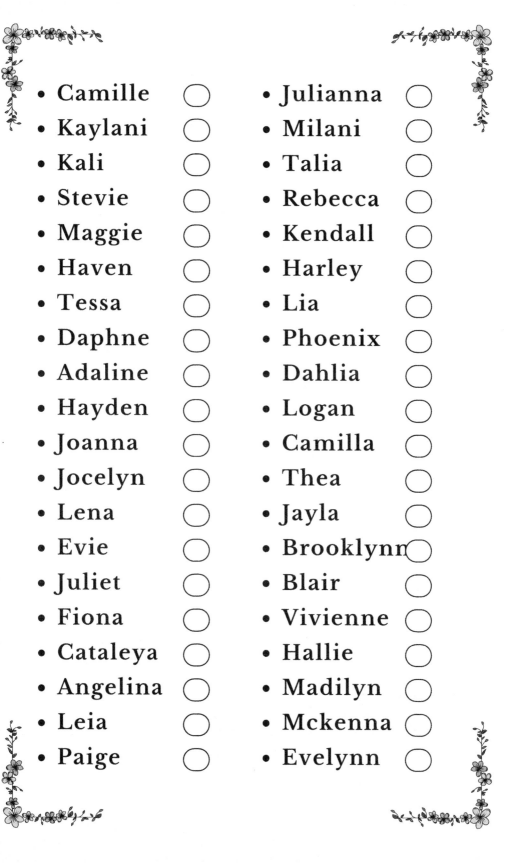

- Camille ◯
- Kaylani ◯
- Kali ◯
- Stevie ◯
- Maggie ◯
- Haven ◯
- Tessa ◯
- Daphne ◯
- Adaline ◯
- Hayden ◯
- Joanna ◯
- Jocelyn ◯
- Lena ◯
- Evie ◯
- Juliet ◯
- Fiona ◯
- Cataleya ◯
- Angelina ◯
- Leia ◯
- Paige ◯

- Julianna ◯
- Milani ◯
- Talia ◯
- Rebecca ◯
- Kendall ◯
- Harley ◯
- Lia ◯
- Phoenix ◯
- Dahlia ◯
- Logan ◯
- Camilla ◯
- Thea ◯
- Jayla ◯
- Brooklynn ◯
- Blair ◯
- Vivienne ◯
- Hallie ◯
- Madilyn ◯
- Mckenna ◯
- Evelynn ◯

- Ophelia ○
- Celeste ○
- Alayah ○
- Winter ○
- Catherine ○
- Collins ○
- Nina ○
- Briella ○
- Palmer ○
- Noa ○
- Mckenzie ○
- Kiara ○
- Amari ○
- Adriana ○
- Gracelynn ○
- Lauren ○
- Cali ○
- Kalani ○
- Aniyah ○
- Nicole ○

- Alexis ○
- Mariah ○
- Gabriela ○
- Wynter ○
- Amina ○
- Ariyah ○
- Adelynn ○
- Remington ○
- Reign ○
- Alaya ○
- Dream ○
- Alexandria ○
- Willa ○
- Avianna ○
- Makayla ○
- Gracelyn ○
- Elle ○
- Amiyah ○
- Arielle ○
- Elianna ○

- Giselle ○
- Brynn ○
- Ainsley ○
- Aitana ○
- Charli ○
- Demi ○
- Makenna ○
- Rosemary ○
- Danna ○
- Izabella ○
- Lilliana ○
- Melissa ○
- Samara ○
- Lana ○
- Mabel ○
- Everlee ○
- Fatima ○
- Leighton ○
- Esme ○
- Raelyn ○

- Madeleine ○
- Nayeli ○
- Camryn ○
- Kira ○
- Annalise ○
- Selah ○
- Serena ○
- Royalty ○
- Rylie ○
- Celine ○
- Laura ○
- Brinley ○
- Frances ○
- Michelle ○
- Heidi ○
- Rory ○
- Sabrina ○
- Destiny ○
- Gwendolyn ○
- Alessandra ○

- Poppy ◯
- Amora ◯
- Nylah ◯
- Luciana ◯
- Maisie ◯
- Miracle ◯
- Joy ◯
- Liana ◯
- Raven ◯
- Shiloh ◯
- Allie ◯
- Daleyza ◯
- Kate ◯
- Lyric ◯
- Alicia ◯
- Lexi ◯
- Addilyn ◯
- Anaya ◯
- Malani ◯
- Paislee ◯

- Elisa ◯
- Kayleigh ◯
- Azalea ◯
- Francesca ◯
- Jordan ◯
- Regina ◯
- Viviana ◯
- Aylin ◯
- Skye ◯
- Daniella ◯
- Makenzie ◯
- Veronica ◯
- Legacy ◯
- Maia ◯
- Ariah ◯
- Alessia ◯
- Carmen ◯
- Astrid ◯
- Maren ◯
- Helen ◯

- Felicity ◯
- Alexa ◯
- Danielle ◯
- Lorelei ◯
- Paris ◯
- Adelina ◯
- Bianca ◯
- Gabrielle ◯
- Jazlyn ◯
- Scarlet ◯
- Bristol ◯
- Navy ◯
- Esmeralda ◯
- Colette ◯
- Stephanie ◯
- Jolene ◯
- Marlee ◯
- Sarai ◯
- Hattie ◯
- Nadia ◯

- Rosie ◯
- Kamryn ◯
- Kenzie ◯
- Alora ◯
- Holly ◯
- Matilda ◯
- Sylvia ◯
- Cameron ◯
- Armani ◯
- Emelia ◯
- Keira ◯
- Braelynn ◯
- Jacqueline ◯
- Alison ◯
- Amanda ◯
- Cassidy ◯
- Emory ◯
- Ari ◯
- Haisley ◯
- Jimena ◯

- Jessica ○
- Elaine ○
- Dorothy ○
- Mira ○
- Eve ○
- Oaklee ○
- Averie ○
- Charleigh ○
- Lyra ○
- Madelynn ○
- Angel ○
- Edith ○
- Jennifer ○
- Raya ○
- Ryan ○
- Heaven ○
- Kyla ○
- Wrenley ○
- Meadow ○
- Carter ○

- Kora ○
- Saige ○
- Kinley ○
- Maci ○
- Mae ○
- Salem ○
- Aisha ○
- Adley ○
- Carolina ○
- Sierra ○
- Alma ○
- Helena ○
- Bonnie ○
- Mylah ○
- Briar ○
- Aurelia ○
- Leona ○
- Macie ○
- Maddison ○
- April ○

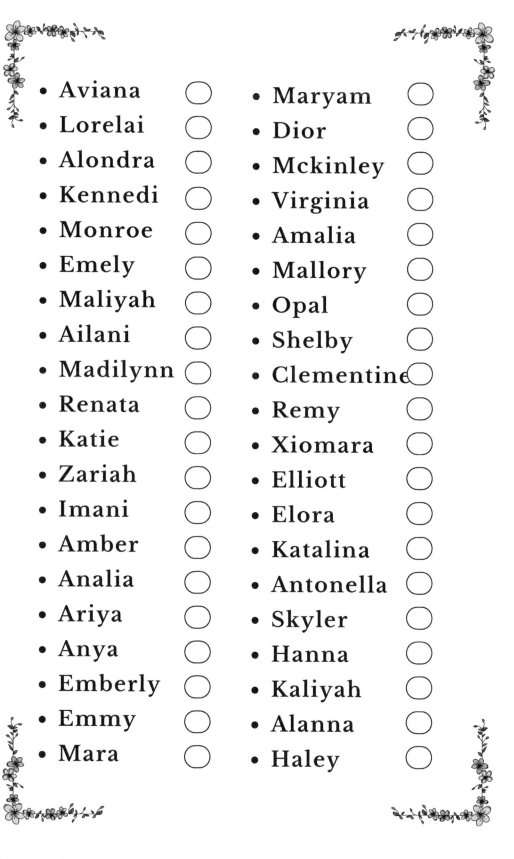

- Aviana ○
- Lorelai ○
- Alondra ○
- Kennedi ○
- Monroe ○
- Emely ○
- Maliyah ○
- Ailani ○
- Madilynn ○
- Renata ○
- Katie ○
- Zariah ○
- Imani ○
- Amber ○
- Analia ○
- Ariya ○
- Anya ○
- Emberly ○
- Emmy ○
- Mara ○

- Maryam ○
- Dior ○
- Mckinley ○
- Virginia ○
- Amalia ○
- Mallory ○
- Opal ○
- Shelby ○
- Clementine ○
- Remy ○
- Xiomara ○
- Elliott ○
- Elora ○
- Katalina ○
- Antonella ○
- Skyler ○
- Hanna ○
- Kaliyah ○
- Alanna ○
- Haley ○

- Itzel ◯
- Cecelia ◯
- Jayleen ◯
- Kensley ◯
- Beatrice ◯
- Journi ◯
- Dylan ◯
- Ivory ◯
- Yaretzi ◯
- Meredith ◯
- Sasha ◯
- Gloria ◯
- Oaklyn ◯
- Sloan ◯
- Abby ◯
- Davina ◯
- Lylah ◯
- Erin ◯
- Reyna ◯
- Kaitlyn ◯

- Michaela ◯
- Nia ◯
- Fernanda ◯
- Jaliyah ◯
- Jenna ◯
- Sylvie ◯
- Miranda ◯
- Anne ◯
- Mina ◯
- Myra ◯
- Aleena ◯
- Alia ◯
- Frankie ◯
- Ellis ◯
- Kathryn ◯
- Nalani ◯
- Nola ◯
- Jemma ◯
- Lennox ◯
- Marie ◯

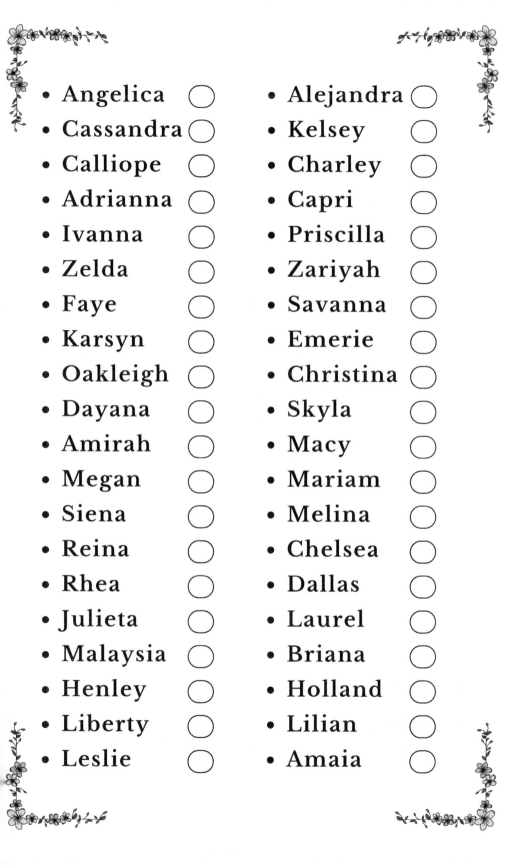

- Angelica ◯
- Cassandra ◯
- Calliope ◯
- Adrianna ◯
- Ivanna ◯
- Zelda ◯
- Faye ◯
- Karsyn ◯
- Oakleigh ◯
- Dayana ◯
- Amirah ◯
- Megan ◯
- Siena ◯
- Reina ◯
- Rhea ◯
- Julieta ◯
- Malaysia ◯
- Henley ◯
- Liberty ◯
- Leslie ◯

- Alejandra ◯
- Kelsey ◯
- Charley ◯
- Capri ◯
- Priscilla ◯
- Zariyah ◯
- Savanna ◯
- Emerie ◯
- Christina ◯
- Skyla ◯
- Macy ◯
- Mariam ◯
- Melina ◯
- Chelsea ◯
- Dallas ◯
- Laurel ◯
- Briana ◯
- Holland ◯
- Lilian ◯
- Amaia ◯

- Blaire ◯
- Margo ◯
- Louise ◯
- Rosalia ◯
- Aleah ◯
- Bethany ◯
- Flora ◯
- Kylee ◯
- Kendra ◯
- Sunny ◯
- Laney ◯
- Tiana ◯
- Chaya ◯
- Ellianna ◯
- Milan ◯
- Aliana ◯
- Estella ◯
- Julie ◯
- Yara ◯
- Rosa ◯

- Cheyenne ◯
- Emmie ◯
- Carly ◯
- Janelle ◯
- Kyra ◯
- Naya ◯
- Malaya ◯
- Sevyn ◯
- Lina ◯
- Mikayla ◯
- Jayda ◯
- Leyla ◯
- Eileen ◯
- Irene ◯
- Karina ◯
- Aileen ◯
- Aliza ◯
- Kataleya ◯
- Kori ◯
- Indie ◯

- Lara ○
- Romina ○
- Jada ○
- Kimber ○
- Amani ○
- Liv ○
- Treasure ○
- Louisa ○
- Marleigh ○
- Winnie ○
- Kassidy ○
- Noah ○
- Monica ○
- Keilani ○
- Zahra ○
- Zaylee ○
- Hadassah ○
- Jamie ○
- Allyson ○
- Anahi ○

- Maxine ○
- Karla ○
- Khaleesi ○
- Johanna ○
- Penny ○
- Hayley ○
- Marilyn ○
- Della ○
- Freyja ○
- Jazmin ○
- Kenna ○
- Ashlyn ○
- Florence ○
- Ezra ○
- Melany ○
- Murphy ○
- Sky ○
- Marina ○
- Noemi ○
- Coraline ○

- Selene ◯
- Bridget ◯
- Alaiya ◯
- Angie ◯
- Fallon ◯
- Thalia ◯
- Rayna ◯
- Martha ◯
- Halle ◯
- Estrella ◯
- Joelle ◯
- Kinslee ◯
- Roselyn ◯
- Theodora ◯
- Jolie ◯
- Dani ◯
- Elodie ◯
- Halo ◯
- Nala ◯
- Promise ◯

- Justice ◯
- Nellie ◯
- Novah ◯
- Estelle ◯
- Jenesis ◯
- Miley ◯
- Hadlee ◯
- Janiyah ◯
- Waverly ◯
- Braelyn ◯
- Pearl ◯
- Aila ◯
- Katelyn ◯
- Sariyah ◯
- Azariah ◯
- Bexley ◯
- Giana ◯
- Lea ◯
- Cadence ◯
- Mavis ◯

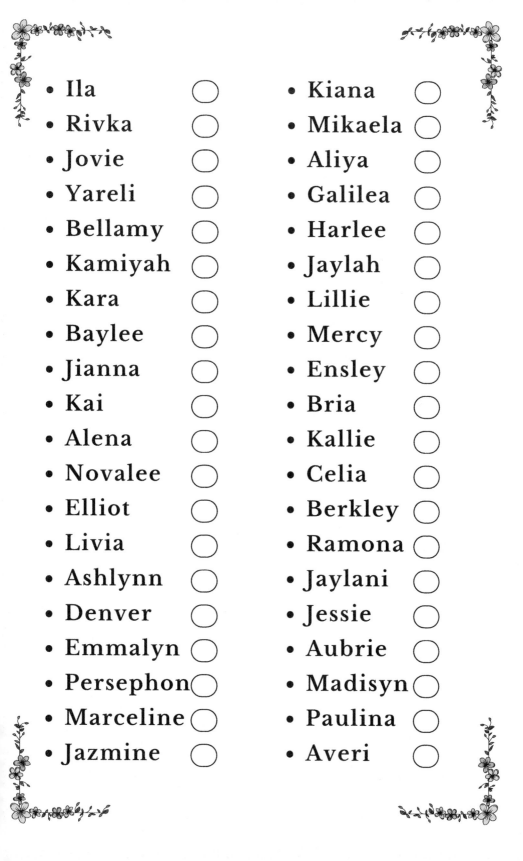

- Ila ◯
- Rivka ◯
- Jovie ◯
- Yareli ◯
- Bellamy ◯
- Kamiyah ◯
- Kara ◯
- Baylee ◯
- Jianna ◯
- Kai ◯
- Alena ◯
- Novalee ◯
- Elliot ◯
- Livia ◯
- Ashlynn ◯
- Denver ◯
- Emmalyn ◯
- Persephon ◯
- Marceline ◯
- Jazmine ◯

- Kiana ◯
- Mikaela ◯
- Aliya ◯
- Galilea ◯
- Harlee ◯
- Jaylah ◯
- Lillie ◯
- Mercy ◯
- Ensley ◯
- Bria ◯
- Kallie ◯
- Celia ◯
- Berkley ◯
- Ramona ◯
- Jaylani ◯
- Jessie ◯
- Aubrie ◯
- Madisyn ◯
- Paulina ◯
- Averi ◯

- Aya ◯
- Chana ◯
- Milana ◯
- Cleo ◯
- Iyla ◯
- Cynthia ◯
- Hana ◯
- Lacey ◯
- Andi ◯
- Giuliana ◯
- Milena ◯
- Leilany ◯
- Saoirse ◯
- Adele ◯
- Drew ◯
- Bailee ◯
- Hunter ◯
- Rayne ◯
- Anais ◯
- Kamari ◯
- Paula ◯
- Rosalee ◯
- Teresa ◯
- Zora ◯
- Avah ◯
- Belen ◯
- Greta ◯
- Layne ◯
- Scout ◯
- Zaniyah ◯
- Amelie ◯
- Dulce ◯
- Chanel ◯
- Clare ◯
- Rebekah ◯
- Giovanna ◯
- Ellison ◯
- Isabela ◯
- Kaydence ◯
- Rosalyn ◯

• Royal	◯	• Avalynn	◯
• Alianna	◯	• Marisol	◯
• August	◯	• Goldie	◯
• Nyra	◯	• Malayah	◯
• Vienna	◯	• Emmeline	◯
• Amoura	◯	• Paloma	◯
• Anika	◯	• Raina	◯
• Harmoni	◯	• Brynleigh	◯
• Kelly	◯	• Chandler	◯
• Linda	◯	• Valery	◯
• Aubriella	◯	• Adalee	◯
• Kairi	◯	• Tinsley	◯
• Ryann	◯	• Violeta	◯
• Avayah	◯	• Baylor	◯
• Gwen	◯	• Lauryn	◯
• Whitley	◯	• Marlowe	◯
• Noor	◯	• Birdie	◯
• Khalani	◯	• Jaycee	◯
• Marianna	◯	• Lexie	◯
• Addyson	◯	• Loretta	◯

- Lilyana ◯
- Princess ◯
- Shay ◯
- Hadleigh ◯
- Natasha ◯
- Indigo ◯
- Zaria ◯
- Addisyn ◯
- Deborah ◯
- Leanna ◯
- Barbara ◯
- Kimora ◯
- Emerald ◯
- Raquel ◯
- Julissa ◯
- Robin ◯
- Austyn ◯
- Dalia ◯
- Nyomi ◯
- Ellen ◯

- Billie ◯
- Haylee ◯
- India ◯
- Kaiya ◯
- Nancy ◯
- Clarissa ◯
- Mazikeen ◯
- Taytum ◯
- Aubrielle ◯
- Rylan ◯
- Ainhoa ◯
- Aspyn ◯
- Elina ◯
- Elsa ◯
- Magdalena ◯
- Kailey ◯
- Arleth ◯
- Joyce ◯
- Judith ◯
- Crystal ◯

- Emberlynn ◯
- Landry ◯
- Paola ◯
- Braylee ◯
- Guinevere ◯
- Aarna ◯
- Aiyana ◯
- Kahlani ◯
- Lyanna ◯
- Sariah ◯
- Itzayana ◯
- Aniya ◯
- Frida ◯
- Jaylene ◯
- Kiera ◯
- Loyalty ◯
- Azaria ◯
- Jaylee ◯
- Kamilah ◯
- Keyla ◯

- Kyleigh ◯
- Micah ◯
- Nataly ◯
- Kathleen ◯
- Zoya ◯
- Meghan ◯
- Soraya ◯
- Zoie ◯
- Arlette ◯
- Zola ◯
- Luisa ◯
- Vida ◯
- Ryder ◯
- Tatiana ◯
- Tori ◯
- Aarya ◯
- Eleanora ◯
- Sandra ◯
- Soleil ◯
- Annabella ◯

Baby Boy Names list

- Liam ◯
- Noah ◯
- Oliver ◯
- Elijah ◯
- James ◯
- William ◯
- Benjamin ◯
- Lucas ◯
- Henry ◯
- Theodore ◯
- Jack ◯
- Levi ◯
- Alexander ◯
- Jackson ◯
- Mateo ◯
- Daniel ◯
- Michael ◯
- Mason ◯
- Sebastian ◯
- Ethan ◯

- Logan ◯
- Owen ◯
- Samuel ◯
- Jacob ◯
- Asher ◯
- Aiden ◯
- John ◯
- Joseph ◯
- Wyatt ◯
- David ◯
- Leo ◯
- Luke ◯
- Julian ◯
- Hudson ◯
- Grayson ◯
- Matthew ◯
- Ezra ◯
- Gabriel ◯
- Carter ◯
- Isaac ◯

- Jayden ○
- Luca ○
- Anthony ○
- Dylan ○
- Lincoln ○
- Thomas ○
- Maverick ○
- Elias ○
- Josiah ○
- Charles ○
- Caleb ○
- Christophe ○
- Ezekiel ○
- Miles ○
- Jaxon ○
- Isaiah ○
- Andrew ○
- Joshua ○
- Nathan ○
- Nolan ○

- Adrian ○
- Cameron ○
- Santiago ○
- Eli ○
- Aaron ○
- Ryan ○
- Angel ○
- Cooper ○
- Waylon ○
- Easton ○
- Kai ○
- Christian ○
- Landon ○
- Colton ○
- Roman ○
- Axel ○
- Brooks ○
- Jonathan ○
- Robert ○
- Jameson ○

- Ian ◯
- Everett ◯
- Greyson ◯
- Wesley ◯
- Jeremiah ◯
- Hunter ◯
- Leonardo ◯
- Jordan ◯
- Jose ◯
- Bennett ◯
- Silas ◯
- Nicholas ◯
- Parker ◯
- Beau ◯
- Weston ◯
- Austin ◯
- Connor ◯
- Carson ◯
- Dominic ◯
- Xavier ◯

- Jaxson ◯
- Jace ◯
- Emmett ◯
- Adam ◯
- Declan ◯
- Rowan ◯
- Micah ◯
- Kayden ◯
- Gael ◯
- River ◯
- Ryder ◯
- Kingston ◯
- Damian ◯
- Sawyer ◯
- Luka ◯
- Evan ◯
- Vincent ◯
- Legend ◯
- Myles ◯
- Harrison ◯

- August ◯
- Bryson ◯
- Amir ◯
- Giovanni ◯
- Chase ◯
- Diego ◯
- Milo ◯
- Jasper ◯
- Walker ◯
- Jason ◯
- Brayden ◯
- Cole ◯
- Nathaniel ◯
- George ◯
- Lorenzo ◯
- Zion ◯
- Luis ◯
- Archer ◯
- Enzo ◯
- Jonah ◯

- Thiago ◯
- Theo ◯
- Ayden ◯
- Zachary ◯
- Calvin ◯
- Braxton ◯
- Ashton ◯
- Rhett ◯
- Atlas ◯
- Jude ◯
- Bentley ◯
- Carlos ◯
- Ryker ◯
- Adriel ◯
- Arthur ◯
- Ace ◯
- Tyler ◯
- Jayce ◯
- Max ◯
- Elliot ◯

- Graham ○
- Kaiden ○
- Maxwell ○
- Juan ○
- Dean ○
- Matteo ○
- Malachi ○
- Ivan ○
- Elliott ○
- Jesus ○
- Emiliano ○
- Messiah ○
- Gavin ○
- Maddox ○
- Camden ○
- Hayden ○
- Leon ○
- Antonio ○
- Justin ○
- Tucker ○

- Brandon ○
- Kevin ○
- Judah ○
- Finn ○
- King ○
- Brody ○
- Xander ○
- Nicolas ○
- Charlie ○
- Arlo ○
- Emmanuel ○
- Barrett ○
- Felix ○
- Alex ○
- Miguel ○
- Abel ○
- Alan ○
- Beckett ○
- Amari ○
- Karter ○

- Timothy ○
- Abraham ○
- Jesse ○
- Zayden ○
- Blake ○
- Alejandro ○
- Dawson ○
- Tristan ○
- Victor ○
- Avery ○
- Joel ○
- Grant ○
- Eric ○
- Patrick ○
- Peter ○
- Richard ○
- Edward ○
- Andres ○
- Emilio ○
- Colt ○

- Knox ○
- Beckham ○
- Adonis ○
- Kyrie ○
- Matias ○
- Oscar ○
- Lukas ○
- Marcus ○
- Hayes ○
- Caden ○
- Remington ○
- Griffin ○
- Nash ○
- Israel ○
- Steven ○
- Holden ○
- Rafael ○
- Zane ○
- Jeremy ○
- Kash ○

- Zayn ◯
- Malcolm ◯
- Kayson ◯
- Bodhi ◯
- Bryan ◯
- Aidan ◯
- Cohen ◯
- Brian ◯
- Cayden ◯
- Andre ◯
- Niko ◯
- Maximilian ◯
- Zander ◯
- Khalil ◯
- Rory ◯
- Francisco ◯
- Cruz ◯
- Kobe ◯
- Reid ◯
- Daxton ◯

- Derek ◯
- Martin ◯
- Jensen ◯
- Karson ◯
- Tate ◯
- Muhammad ◯
- Jaden ◯
- Joaquin ◯
- Josue ◯
- Gideon ◯
- Dante ◯
- Cody ◯
- Bradley ◯
- Orion ◯
- Spencer ◯
- Angelo ◯
- Erick ◯
- Jaylen ◯
- Julius ◯
- Manuel ◯

- Ellis ◯
- Colson ◯
- Cairo ◯
- Gunner ◯
- Wade ◯
- Chance ◯
- Odin ◯
- Anderson ◯
- Kane ◯
- Raymond ◯
- Cristian ◯
- Aziel ◯
- Prince ◯
- Ezequiel ◯
- Jake ◯
- Otto ◯
- Eduardo ◯
- Rylan ◯
- Ali ◯
- Cade ◯

- Stephen ◯
- Ari ◯
- Kameron ◯
- Dakota ◯
- Warren ◯
- Ricardo ◯
- Killian ◯
- Mario ◯
- Romeo ◯
- Cyrus ◯
- Ismael ◯
- Russell ◯
- Tyson ◯
- Edwin ◯
- Desmond ◯
- Nasir ◯
- Remy ◯
- Tanner ◯
- Fernando ◯
- Hector ◯

- Titus ◯
- Lawson ◯
- Sean ◯
- Kyle ◯
- Elian ◯
- Corbin ◯
- Bowen ◯
- Wilder ◯
- Armani ◯
- Royal ◯
- Stetson ◯
- Briggs ◯
- Sullivan ◯
- Leonel ◯
- Callan ◯
- Finnegan ◯
- Jay ◯
- Zayne ◯
- Marshall ◯
- Kade ◯

- Travis ◯
- Sterling ◯
- Raiden ◯
- Sergio ◯
- Tatum ◯
- Cesar ◯
- Zyaire ◯
- Milan ◯
- Devin ◯
- Gianni ◯
- Kamari ◯
- Royce ◯
- Malik ◯
- Jared ◯
- Franklin ◯
- Clark ◯
- Noel ◯
- Marco ◯
- Archie ◯
- Apollo ◯

- Pablo ◯
- Garrett ◯
- Oakley ◯
- Memphis ◯
- Quinn ◯
- Onyx ◯
- Alijah ◯
- Baylor ◯
- Edgar ◯
- Nehemiah ◯
- Winston ◯
- Major ◯
- Rhys ◯
- Forrest ◯
- Jaiden ◯
- Reed ◯
- Santino ◯
- Troy ◯
- Caiden ◯
- Harvey ◯

- Collin ◯
- Solomon ◯
- Donovan ◯
- Damon ◯
- Jeffrey ◯
- Kason ◯
- Sage ◯
- Grady ◯
- Kendrick ◯
- Leland ◯
- Luciano ◯
- Pedro ◯
- Hank ◯
- Hugo ◯
- Esteban ◯
- Johnny ◯
- Kashton ◯
- Ronin ◯
- Ford ◯
- Mathias ◯

- Porter ○
- Erik ○
- Johnathan ○
- Frank ○
- Tripp ○
- Casey ○
- Fabian ○
- Leonidas ○
- Baker ○
- Matthias ○
- Philip ○
- Jayceon ○
- Kian ○
- Saint ○
- Ibrahim ○
- Jaxton ○
- Augustus ○
- Callen ○
- Trevor ○
- Ruben ○

- Adan ○
- Conor ○
- Dax ○
- Braylen ○
- Kaison ○
- Francis ○
- Kyson ○
- Andy ○
- Lucca ○
- Mack ○
- Peyton ○
- Alexis ○
- Deacon ○
- Kasen ○
- Kamden ○
- Frederick ○
- Princeton ○
- Braylon ○
- Wells ○
- Nikolai ○

- Iker ◯
- Bo ◯
- Dominick ◯
- Moshe ◯
- Cassius ◯
- Gregory ◯
- Lewis ◯
- Kieran ◯
- Isaias ◯
- Seth ◯
- Marcos ◯
- Omari ◯
- Shane ◯
- Keegan ◯
- Jase ◯
- Asa ◯
- Sonny ◯
- Uriel ◯
- Pierce ◯
- Jasiah ◯

- Eden ◯
- Rocco ◯
- Banks ◯
- Cannon ◯
- Denver ◯
- Zaiden ◯
- Roberto ◯
- Shawn ◯
- Drew ◯
- Emanuel ◯
- Kolton ◯
- Ayaan ◯
- Ares ◯
- Conner ◯
- Jalen ◯
- Alonzo ◯
- Enrique ◯
- Dalton ◯
- Moses ◯
- Koda ◯

- Bodie ○
- Jamison ○
- Phillip ○
- Zaire ○
- Jonas ○
- Kylo ○
- Moises ○
- Shepherd ○
- Allen ○
- Kenzo ○
- Mohamed ○
- Keanu ○
- Dexter ○
- Conrad ○
- Bruce ○
- Sylas ○
- Soren ○
- Raphael ○
- Rowen ○
- Gunnar ○

- Sutton ○
- Quentin ○
- Jaziel ○
- Emmitt ○
- Makai ○
- Koa ○
- Maximilian ○
- Brixton ○
- Dariel ○
- Zachariah ○
- Roy ○
- Armando ○
- Corey ○
- Saul ○
- Izaiah ○
- Danny ○
- Davis ○
- Ridge ○
- Yusuf ○
- Ariel ○

• Shiloh	◯	• Boston	◯
• Arjun	◯	• Axton	◯
• Marcelo	◯	• Amos	◯
• Abram	◯	• Chandler	◯
• Benson	◯	• Leandro	◯
• Huxley	◯	• Raul	◯
• Nikolas	◯	• Scott	◯
• Zain	◯	• Reign	◯
• Kohen	◯	• Alessandro	◯
• Samson	◯	• Camilo	◯
• Miller	◯	• Derrick	◯
• Donald	◯	• Morgan	◯
• Finnley	◯	• Julio	◯
• Kannon	◯	• Clay	◯
• Lucian	◯	• Edison	◯
• Watson	◯	• Jaime	◯
• Keith	◯	• Augustine	◯
• Westin	◯	• Julien	◯
• Tadeo	◯	• Zeke	◯
• Sincere	◯	• Marvin	◯

- Bellamy ○
- Landen ○
- Dustin ○
- Jamie ○
- Krew ○
- Kyree ○
- Colter ○
- Johan ○
- Houston ○
- Layton ○
- Quincy ○
- Case ○
- Atreus ○
- Cayson ○
- Aarav ○
- Darius ○
- Harlan ○
- Justice ○
- Abdiel ○
- Layne ○

- Raylan ○
- Arturo ○
- Taylor ○
- Anakin ○
- Ander ○
- Hamza ○
- Otis ○
- Azariah ○
- Leonard ○
- Colby ○
- Duke ○
- Flynn ○
- Trey ○
- Gustavo ○
- Fletcher ○
- Issac ○
- Sam ○
- Trenton ○
- Callahan ○
- Chris ○

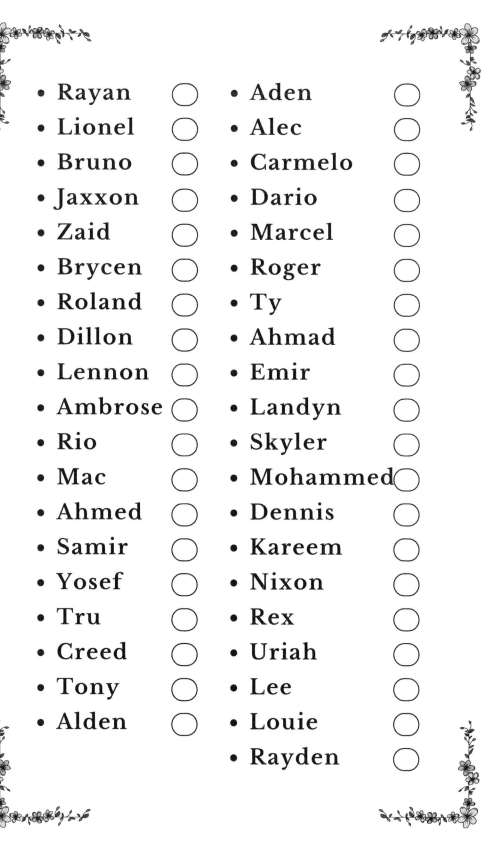

- Rayan ○
- Lionel ○
- Bruno ○
- Jaxxon ○
- Zaid ○
- Brycen ○
- Roland ○
- Dillon ○
- Lennon ○
- Ambrose ○
- Rio ○
- Mac ○
- Ahmed ○
- Samir ○
- Yosef ○
- Tru ○
- Creed ○
- Tony ○
- Alden ○

- Aden ○
- Alec ○
- Carmelo ○
- Dario ○
- Marcel ○
- Roger ○
- Ty ○
- Ahmad ○
- Emir ○
- Landyn ○
- Skyler ○
- Mohammed ○
- Dennis ○
- Kareem ○
- Nixon ○
- Rex ○
- Uriah ○
- Lee ○
- Louie ○
- Rayden ○

- Reese ◯
- Alberto ◯
- Cason ◯
- Quinton ◯
- Kingsley ◯
- Chaim ◯
- Alfredo ◯
- Mauricio ◯
- Caspian ◯
- Legacy ◯
- Ocean ◯
- Ozzy ◯
- Briar ◯
- Wilson ◯
- Forest ◯
- Grey ◯
- Joziah ◯
- Salem ◯
- Neil ◯
- Remi ◯

- Bridger ◯
- Harry ◯
- Jefferson ◯
- Lachlan ◯
- Nelson ◯
- Casen ◯
- Salvador ◯
- Magnus ◯
- Tommy ◯
- Marcellus ◯
- Maximo ◯
- Jerry ◯
- Clyde ◯
- Aron ◯
- Keaton ◯
- Eliam ◯
- Lian ◯
- Trace ◯
- Douglas ◯
- Junior ◯

- Reese ◯
- Alberto ◯
- Cason ◯
- Quinton ◯
- Kingsley ◯
- Chaim ◯
- Alfredo ◯
- Mauricio ◯
- Caspian ◯
- Legacy ◯
- Ocean ◯
- Ozzy ◯
- Briar ◯
- Wilson ◯
- Forest ◯
- Grey ◯
- Joziah ◯
- Salem ◯
- Neil ◯
- Remi ◯

- Titan ◯
- Cullen ◯
- Cillian ◯
- Musa ◯
- Mylo ◯
- Hugh ◯
- Tomas ◯
- Vincenzo ◯
- Westley ◯
- Langston ◯
- Byron ◯
- Kiaan ◯
- Loyal ◯
- Orlando ◯
- Kyro ◯
- Amias ◯
- Amiri ◯
- Jimmy ◯
- Vicente ◯
- Khari ◯

- Brendan ◯
- Rey ◯
- Ben ◯
- Emery ◯
- Zyair ◯
- Bjorn ◯
- Evander ◯
- Ramon ◯
- Alvin ◯
- Ricky ◯
- Jagger ◯
- Brock ◯
- Dakari ◯
- Eddie ◯
- Blaze ◯
- Gatlin ◯
- Alonso ◯
- Curtis ◯
- Kylian ◯
- Nathanael ◯

- Devon ◯
- Wayne ◯
- Zakai ◯
- Mathew ◯
- Rome ◯
- Riggs ◯
- Aryan ◯
- Avi ◯
- Hassan ◯
- Lochlan ◯
- Stanley ◯
- Dash ◯
- Kaiser ◯
- Benicio ◯
- Bryant ◯
- Talon ◯
- Rohan ◯
- Wesson ◯
- Joe ◯
- Noe ◯

- Melvin ◯
- Vihaan ◯
- Zayd ◯
- Darren ◯
- Enoch ◯
- Mitchell ◯
- Jedidiah ◯
- Brodie ◯
- Castiel ◯
- Ira ◯
- Lance ◯
- Guillermo ◯
- Thatcher ◯
- Ermias ◯
- Misael ◯
- Jakari ◯
- Emory ◯
- Mccoy ◯
- Rudy ◯
- Thaddeus ◯

- Valentin ◯
- Yehuda ◯
- Bode ◯
- Madden ◯
- Kase ◯
- Bear ◯
- Boden ◯
- Jiraiya ◯
- Maurice ◯
- Alvaro ◯
- Ameer ◯
- Demetrius ◯
- Eliseo ◯
- Kabir ◯
- Kellan ◯
- Allan ◯
- Azrael ◯
- Calum ◯
- Niklaus ◯
- Ray ◯

- Damari ○
- Elio ○
- Jon ○
- Leighton ○
- Axl ○
- Dane ○
- Eithan ○
- Eugene ○
- Kenji ○
- Jakob ○
- Colten ○
- Eliel ○
- Nova ○
- Santos ○
- Zahir ○
- Idris ○
- Ishaan ○
- Kole ○
- Korbin ○
- Seven ○

- Alaric ○
- Kellen ○
- Bronson ○
- Franco ○
- Wes ○
- Larry ○
- Mekhi ○
- Jamal ○
- Dilan ○
- Elisha ○
- Brennan ○
- Kace ○
- Van ○
- Felipe ○
- Fisher ○
- Cal ○
- Dior ○
- Judson ○
- Alfonso ○
- Deandre ○

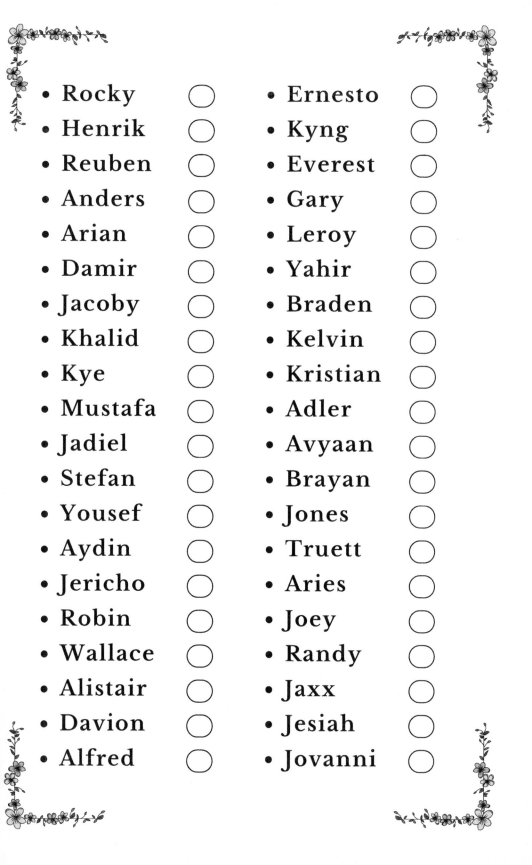

- Rocky ◯
- Henrik ◯
- Reuben ◯
- Anders ◯
- Arian ◯
- Damir ◯
- Jacoby ◯
- Khalid ◯
- Kye ◯
- Mustafa ◯
- Jadiel ◯
- Stefan ◯
- Yousef ◯
- Aydin ◯
- Jericho ◯
- Robin ◯
- Wallace ◯
- Alistair ◯
- Davion ◯
- Alfred ◯

- Ernesto ◯
- Kyng ◯
- Everest ◯
- Gary ◯
- Leroy ◯
- Yahir ◯
- Braden ◯
- Kelvin ◯
- Kristian ◯
- Adler ◯
- Avyaan ◯
- Brayan ◯
- Jones ◯
- Truett ◯
- Aries ◯
- Joey ◯
- Randy ◯
- Jaxx ◯
- Jesiah ◯
- Jovanni ◯

- Azriel ◯
- Brecken ◯
- Harley ◯
- Zechariah ◯
- Gordon ◯
- Jakai ◯
- Carl ◯
- Graysen ◯
- Kylen ◯
- Ayan ◯
- Branson ◯
- Crosby ◯
- Dominik ◯
- Jabari ◯
- Jaxtyn ◯
- Kristopher ◯
- Ulises ◯
- Zyon ◯
- Fox ◯
- Howard ◯

- Salvatore ◯
- Turner ◯
- Vance ◯
- Harlem ◯
- Jair ◯
- Jakobe ◯
- Jeremias ◯
- Osiris ◯
- Azael ◯
- Bowie ◯
- Canaan ◯
- Elon ◯
- Granger ◯
- Karsyn ◯
- Zavier ◯
- Cain ◯
- Dangelo ◯
- Heath ◯
- Yisroel ◯
- Gian ◯

- Shepard ○
- Harold ○
- Kamdyn ○
- Rene ○
- Rodney ○
- Yaakov ○
- Adrien ○
- Kartier ○
- Cassian ○
- Coleson ○
- Ahmir ○
- Darian ○
- Genesis ○
- Kalel ○
- Agustin ○
- Wylder ○
- Yadiel ○
- Ephraim ○
- Kody ○
- Neo ○

- Ignacio ○
- Osman ○
- Aldo ○
- Abdullah ○
- Cory ○
- Blaine ○
- Dimitri ○
- Khai ○
- Landry ○
- Palmer ○
- Benedict ○
- Leif ○
- Koen ○
- Maxton ○
- Mordechai ○
- Zev ○
- Atharv ○
- Bishop ○
- Blaise ○
- Davian ○

Girl Names Ending in A

- Alexa ◯
- Amelia ◯
- Anna ◯
- Aria ◯
- Ariana ◯
- Aurora ◯
- Ava ◯
- Bella ◯
- Camila ◯
- Elena ◯
- Ella ◯
- Emma ◯
- Gabriella ◯
- Isabella ◯
- Julia ◯
- Layla ◯
- Luna ◯
- Maya ◯
- Mia ◯
- Mila

- Nora ◯
- Olivia ◯
- Samantha ◯
- Sophia/Sofia ◯
- Stella ◯
- Victoria ◯
- Zara ◯

Boy Names Ending in A

- Akira ◯
- Asa ◯
- Cuba ◯
- Dakota ◯
- Dana ◯
- Elisha ◯
- Ezra ◯
- Hamza ◯
- Hosea ◯
- Ilya ◯
- Indiana ◯
- Ira ◯
- Koa ◯
- Koda ◯
- Joshua ◯
- Luca ◯
- Misha ◯
- Musa ◯
- Mustafa ◯
- Nicola ◯

- Nikita ◯
- Nova ◯
- Pasha ◯
- Santana ◯
- Sasha/Sascha ◯
- Seneca ◯
- Sequoia ◯
- Vanya ◯
- Yehuda ◯

Girl Names Ending in N

- Addison ◯
- Adelyn ◯
- Allison ◯
- Autumn ◯
- Brooklyn ◯
- Eden ◯
- Emerson ◯
- Evelyn ◯
- Hayden ◯
- Jocelyn ◯
- Jordyn ◯
- Lauren ◯
- Lillian ◯
- Lynn ◯
- London ◯
- Madelyn ◯
- Madison ◯
- Morgan ◯
- Payton ◯

- Quinn ◯
- Raelynn ◯
- Reagan ◯
- Rowan ◯
- Teagan ◯
- Vivian ◯

Boy Names Ending in N

- Aaron ◯
- Adrian/Adrien ◯
- Benjamin ◯
- Cameron ◯
- Carson ◯
- Christian ◯
- Colton ◯
- Dylan ◯
- Easton ◯
- Ethan ◯
- Grayson ◯
- Hudson ◯
- Jackson/Jaxon ◯
- Jayden ◯
- John/Jonathan ◯
- Julian ◯
- Landon ◯
- Lincoln ◯
- Logan ◯
- Mason ◯
- Nathan ◯
- Nolan ◯
- Owen ◯
- Ryan ◯
- Sebastian ◯

Girl Names Ending in Y

- Ashley ◯
- Aubrey ◯
- Audrey ◯
- Avery ◯
- Bailey ◯
- Emery ◯
- Emily ◯
- Everly ◯
- Finley ◯
- Hadley ◯
- Hailey ◯
- Ivy ◯
- Kennedy ◯
- Kimberly ◯
- Kinsley ◯
- Lilly/Lily ◯
- Lucy ◯
- Mary ◯
- Melody ◯
- Paisley ◯

- Riley ◯
- Ruby ◯
- Serenity ◯
- Sydney ◯
- Trinity ◯
- Zoey ◯

Boy Names Ending in Y

- Andy ◯
- Anthony ◯
- Avery ◯
- Bentley ◯
- Bradley ◯
- Brady ◯
- Brantley ◯
- Brody ◯
- Cody ◯
- Corey ◯
- Finley ◯
- Grady ◯
- Gregory ◯
- Harvey ◯
- Henry ◯
- Jay ◯
- Jeffrey ◯
- Jeremy ◯
- Johnny ◯
- Oakley ◯

- Riley ◯
- Rory ◯
- Timothy ◯
- Troy ◯
- Wesley ◯
- Zachary ◯

SEARCH IT

NAME MEANING SEARCH TOOL :

THE DOMAIN MEAN

The first thing that you need to do is research your baby's name with the purpose of finding out if the domain name is available, then you may want to skip this step if technology is not an important factor for you. But for some parents, a baby's domain name can really have a powerful effect on their brand, and is an integral part of the identity they chose for their baby.

A domain name is a string that identifies a realm of administrative autonomy, authority or control within the Internet. Domain names are often used to identify services provided through the Internet, such as websites, email services and more. As of 2017.

SEARCH FOR A DOMAIN NAME

Choosing a Baby Name

Work Pages

Inspiration

What / Who Is Important To You And Your Family ?

....
....
....
....
....

What Inspires You

....
....
....
....
....

What Do You Want Your Baby's Name To Represent ?

....
....
....
....
....

Boy Names

Gigl Names

....

....

....

....

....

....

....

....

....

....

....

....

....

....

....

....

....

....

....

....

....

....

....

....

....

....

Write it

Full Name

....

Possible Nicknames

....

....

Initials

....

Full Name

....

Possible Nicknames

....

....

Initials

....

Search iT

Name

....

What Does The Name Mean

....

....

Is The Domain Avaiable

....

Name

....

What Does The Name Mean

....

....

Is The Domain Avaiable

....

Why we chose your name

Your Full Name

....

Your Nicknames

....

What Does Your Name Mean

....

....

....

Why We Chose Your Name

....

....

....

Other Name We Considered

....

....

....

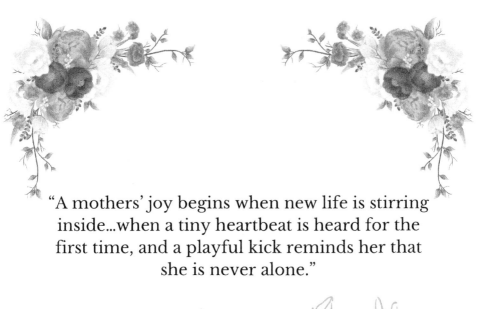

"A mothers' joy begins when new life is stirring inside...when a tiny heartbeat is heard for the first time, and a playful kick reminds her that she is never alone."

I HOPE THIS BOOK HELPED YOU, I'D LOVE TO HEAR YOUR HONEST OPINION

★ ★ ★ ★ ★

Printed in Great Britain
by Amazon

15325490R00047